GROWING UP IN THE COLONIAL

A memoir by

EDWIN LIGHT

Copyrighted Material
Growing Up in the Colonial
Copyright © 2021. Edwin Light. All Rights Reserved.

No part of this publication may be reproduced, stored in a retrieval system or transmitted, in any form or by any means—electronic, mechanical, photocopy, recording, or otherwise—without prior written permission from the publisher, except for the inclusion of brief quotations in a review.

For information about this title or to order other books and/or electronic media, contact the publisher:

Edwin Light
email: ehlight40@gmail.com

ISBN
979-8-9853135-0-5 (Paperback)
979-8-9853135-1-2 (eBook)

Printed in the United States of America

Cover and Interior design: Van-Garde Imagery, Inc.

Cover Photo: l-r, Steve Kovsky, neighbor, Jake, behind screen door, one of three colored employees, and the Hood family, George T. Hood, Proprietor, circa 1916.

My Mother and my Grandmother guided me through my childhood and beyond, encouraging and inspiring me to do my best. I dedicate this book to them.

Mother and me outside the entrance to the hotel, 1941

In the 1940s and 50s I grew up in our family's hotel. The changing cast of characters informed and fascinated me every day, like the gluttonous salesman, the boarder with shrapnel, the deputy sheriff and dynamite, and Professor Kerns at the piano. And of course, our family, including Mother and her trumpet, Uncle Howard and the latest gossip, mischievous me, and Aunt Missouri's left eye. All this unfolded in my grandpa's creation, the Colonial Hotel.

After two terms as the Polk County Sheriff and an unsuccessful run for a third term, my Grandpa George Tate Hood contemplated his next opportunity, and he didn't have to look beyond Polk County in southeastern Tennessee. He was already acquainted with the burgeoning economy in Copperhill, where the Tennessee Copper Company was expanding its operations, six Louisville & Nashville passenger trains were steaming through town every day and commercial buildings were filling up what had been farmers' fields.

My enterprising Grandpa recognized the need for lodging and meals for TCC's employees. He wisely chose a site at the main entrance to Copperhill across from the L&N railroad station, a location that was within walking distance of the copper smelters. In 1913 construction of the Colonial began, and he moved his wife Lillie and their seven children to Copperhill, my mother Frankie among them.

Hood Family portrait, hotel lobby, circa 1914
l-r standing, Frankie, Fred, Katie, Oliver, and Howard; l-r seated, George /Grandpa and Luford, Lillie/Grandma and Rena/nicknamed 'Shine'

The *Polk County Republican* reported in February 1914, "He [George T. Hood] has new furnishings throughout, hot and cold water, bathrooms, fresh spring water, steam heat, etc, and we bespeak for him a liberal patronage." The Colonial could accommodate up to 32 guests in 16 rooms, and more if the Hood children doubled up.

Grandpa had passed on before I came along, but my Grandma happily shared with me many stories about her George. In the parlor, with her silver-gray hair in wavelets, she would lean back on the daybed covered in pink-flowered fabric and enchant me with another tale. That particular day she was expecting company, so she had rouged her cheeks and lips, powdered her face and put on her favorite flowered dress, covering the corset she padded to compensate for sagging breasts. I could smell the *Evening in Paris* she always dabbed behind her ears.

Grandma especially liked to recall the courtship.

"He did what?" I asked.

"He tossed love notes from the train."

"But..." As a kid I couldn't imagine...

"Your Grandpa worked in those days for the Louisville & Nashville railroad. The train didn't stop in Whitestone (Georgia), so he tossed notes off the train. That's how he courted me."

"Grandma, are you pullin my leg?"

"It's true. That's the way we stayed in touch. We had no telephone. George wrote notes and put 'em in a magazine and threw 'em to me." She paused... "How I loved readin' ev'ry word! They'd end somethin' like, 'I'm thinking about you, Lillie,' signed, 'George.' I couldn't wait to read the next one!" Another sigh.

"I wanna see one."

"Good Lord, they're long gone."

I frowned. "Well, what was Grandpa like, what was he really like?"

I have a photo of my grandpa when he was the sheriff surrounded by Polk County officials. His stern demeanor in that picture spooked me as a kid. Mother did point out that her papa had a softer side, "For a Kiwanis parade he dressed as a woman; and a Kiwanian from Nashville complimented his performance." *My Grandpa was in drag? Was my Grandpa something other than a gun-toting macho man?* The answer is no; however, he did wear a girdle.

Next Grandma told me the most exciting story of all. It happened during the construction of the Colonial. With eyes sparkling she recalled,

"George was standin' on the new front porch of the hotel, rowdy as could be, all lickered up with moonshine. Along came Officer Gus Barclay who arrested George for disturbin' the peace. Gus handcuffed your grandpa and dragged him to the jailhouse with George shoutin' all the way, 'You son-of-a-bitch. You're gonna pay.'"

Oh, noooo!

Today I can understand Grandpa's rage. After all, he had been a county sheriff, and now a flatfoot was arresting him!

Grandma smiled as she continued the tale. "It was almost Christmas when your Grandpa crossed paths again with Gus Barclay, near the railroad crossin' in the middle o' town. Gus was talkin' with W.W. Panter.

"George walked on by, nodded to W.W. and said 'Hello,' ignorin' Gus.

"Gus, in a teasin' kinda voice said, 'Hello, George.'

"Your Grandpa snapped back, 'There's no hello for you, you goddamn son-of-a-bitch.' George turned and started to walk away when Gus said,

'Don't you call me that!'

"Gus walked toward George and tried to take hold of his arm.

"George pulled away and out came his gun, 'Don't start anything here!'

"Gus pulled out his gun and shot George in the hip. George spun round, but he didn't fall. Then Gus fired again. This time the bullet struck George right across the chest.

"Your grandpa pointed his pistol and started firin' at Gus. They emptied their guns and tried to fire again, click, click. Gus walked toward George wavin' his gun in the air, but George jerked to the side and struck Gus on top 'is head with the gun butt. Gus, he fell righ' down."

This is more exciting than the westerns I see on Saturdays!

"George dropped beside Gus and hit his head hard several times. T. E. Withrow tried pullin' George offa Gus, but George slipped out and struck Gus again with the butt o' his gun. Gus slouched down and died.

"Your Grandpa was bleedin' a god-awful amount. Doc Jones cleaned him up, and was able to pull out two bullets, but not all. Two were too close to 'is heart and spine. Your Grandpa survived ... after several months at death's door."

The county court reviewed the shootout. Officer Barclay, all sworn witnesses concluded, had deliberately provoked my Grandpa, and fired the first two shots. Grandpa was defending himself. Barclay gambled and lost.

In 1922 my Grandpa died. My Aunt Lon, a nurse, told me years later, "George may have died of too much moonshine, but I believe he died of lead poisonin' from those bullets that never came out."

That thought may have comforted Officer Barclay in his grave.

When a guest arrived at the Colonial, he entered the lobby through a large front door with a glass panel at the top that bore the hotel's name in black letters shadowed in gold. Casement windows on either side of the door, long sealed by paint, featured diamond-shaped lattices on top. The lobby walls were painted beige with dark brown molding and baseboards. The checkered linoleum was hued in black and what had probably been white. But by the time I was doing chores there, no matter how many times we mopped the floor, no one could quite make out the original color.

The guest could see on his right two porcelain sinks where he could wash up before meals. On the floor nearby sat a dark-green metal spittoon that tobacco-chewers dirtied daily.

"Not again!" Starting in the late 1940s it was my task every Saturday morning to clean the spittoons. There were five of them in the lobby. Nothing disgusted me more than wiping them out; but I knew when I finished that yukky task, I could see westerns at the Doradele Theatre. Two westerns for 14 cents with the likes of Gene Autry and Roy Rogers, plus serials with Superman, The Lone Ranger and my favorite, Spider Woman. She crisped her victims in a giant web with the flip of a switch, unless of course someone rescued them at the last possible moment. "Hurry up!" we shouted from the balcony, "She's flippin' the…!"

Beyond the clean spittoon the guest could see the registry window about chest-high where my Mother would greet him, and where he would sign the ledger that spun around on a ball-bearing platform. Close by stood a dome-shaped bell. Family often signed the guest register for the fun of it. My Mother must have been enamored of Hollywood when she wrote in 1923 her screen name, "Miss F. F. Fazenda."

Continuing along the right wall, the guest could see a long, rectangular library table, where there were usually several men seated on well-worn captain's chairs. They would be chatting, smoking Camels and Chesterfields and thumbing through the latest issues of *The Saturday Evening Post* and *Life* magazines. Ash trays and ash stands were scattered around the lobby to accommodate all the smokers.

On the opposite wall, cane-bottomed rockers circled round a pot-bellied stove that glowed red with wood and coal in the winter months. I often watched Mr. Eure, a longtime boarder, rock and tamp his pipe, while others cut off plugs of chewing tobacco. Huddled nearby were large pots filled with snake plants.

To the left of the dining room entrance, the guest saw a three-foot steam-heating radiator, one of many in the hotel that hissed on a winter's day. To the right of the dining room, the guest climbed the stairwell to the second floor and the guest rooms. In a small and simply furnished room, he dropped his bag and saw ahead of him a full-size, iron-frame bed. If he wanted, he washed up with the ceramic pitcher and bowl nestled on top on one of Grandma's embroidered table scarves. He could tuck his clothing in the drawers of the washstand and hang up the rest in the armoire. In the room of Mr. Sneed, a jewelry store owner in town, the armoire held many neckties; he sometimes passed on a few to Grandma for quilting.

At the end of the second-floor hallway stood two porcelain sinks where I sometimes saw Mr. Panter, a night watchman at the copper mines, and other guests shaving. Two bathrooms with porcelain tubs, sinks and toilets were about midway down the hall. Mother told me the tubs during Prohibition were pressed into service for making moonshine. *Bathing or drinking?... What a choice!*

Sometimes, when help was not available, I cleaned the guest bathrooms. That was on top of my regular chores: bell hopping, cleaning the spittoons and shoveling the coal ash out of the furnace.

The ashes, clinkers we called them, were heavy, glowing and red-hot. One day at noontime, with a full dining room above, I was dropping clinkers by the shovelful into a wheelbarrow.

Enough! I'm sick of all the stuff I have to do.

Looking at the smoldering ashes, *I'll show 'em!* I started peeing on the clinkers. The smoke rose up through the floorboards of the kitchen and the dining room. Family, carrying platters of food and drinks, stopped in their tracks, "Where's that awful smell coming from?" No one could find the source, not even Mother.

I sat at the top of the basement stairs reveling in the glory of my protest. *Could I possibly do better than this?*

Then I heard my father ask, "Where's Edwin?"

My mother wrote in our local paper, the *Copper City Advance,* about life in the early years of the hotel. She described her father as "a strict parent and his word was law in the family. The children were not allowed to play or mingle with the hotel guests. Papa erected a partition in the first-floor hallway and the children didn't dare venture past it without his permission."

Grandpa's presence still lingered in the hotel when I came along. "Don't do this, and don't do that," sprang often from my mother's lips. I suffered the same strict discipline she had known as a child. One of my earliest memories, I may have been seven at the time, centered on a small, plastic savings bank.

Mother was pointing her finger and her tongue at me, "You've been a bad, bad boy. You shouldn't have taken the silver dollar to the dime store!"

"I only wanted this penny bank (holding it up) … with a birdie on top."

"No! You took the dollar without asking! Now take the bank back!"

"Noooo, Mommyyyyyy!"

She pointed to the door.

I dragged myself back to Shibley's Five and Dime, sobbing all the way.

A switch would have caused less pain.

Grandpa was also a country fiddler. Cousin George still has his fiddle. *Did he play for square- dancing? Did he play at his wedding on June 4, 1899?* He may have played that day for couples do-si-do-ing in his family's barn.

Whatever the case, Grandpa handed down his musical gene to my Mother. In her teens she began playing the trumpet, but first, a look at her troubled entry into this world.

Mother was born in the Polk County Jailhouse in Benton, Tennessee where Grandpa, the county sheriff, resided with his family. On the front porch of the jailhouse, two of Mother's siblings were fighting over a box of matches while holding her, just eight months old. They were grabbing at each other for the matches, now one succeeded, then the other. In the tussle they forgot to hang on to Mother, who tumbled onto the plank floor, breaking her left elbow and wrist. That night she made no sounds; no one knew she was injured. It wasn't until the next morning when Grandma lifted Mother out of bed that she cried. Three doctors treated her in

1909, even breaking and resetting the limb; her left arm and hand, however, remained twisted and almost useless for the rest of her life.

As a 'cripple,' Mother was relegated to the ironing room out of sight of the hotel guests. In public school, she lamented that the other children wouldn't hold her left hand when playing games. As a young girl she sang in church a song that revealed the depth of her feelings:

> "Mama, when I go to Heaven,
> Will the angels let me play?
>
> Just because I am a cripple, Will
> they say I'm in the way?
>
> Here the children never want me,
> I'm a bother they all say.
>
> Mama, when I go to Heaven, Will
> the angels let me play?"

Grandpa became Mother's champion. "I was his favorite," she told me. Grandpa bought her a trumpet when she showed some interest and talent for the instrument; and he paid for her trumpet lessons. The more she played, the more she was identified with her instrument. Soon family began calling her "Tootsie." The name stuck. Cousins still remember her with her short-cropped dark brown hair as Aunt Tootsie.

In the 1930s through the 1940s Mother played in several musical ensembles, including an all-girl orchestra, the Knights of Pythias Band and the Copper Basin Band. She even played in a barroom where she tired of repeating "I'm Forever Blowing Bubbles."

Mother had escaped the ironing room forever. The trumpet sounded her worth.

Mother, 2nd row, third from right, was one of only two women in the Copper Basin Band, 1930s.

I started piano lessons at age five with Mother's friend, Professor Fred Kerns. Cousin Herbert called the Professor "Billy Goat" because of his goatee. Kerns was probably in his fifties, amiable and generous with praise.

After a few lessons I went with Mother to First Methodist, where Kerns' other students were performing a recital. When the program ended, much to my surprise, the gray-haired Kerns turned to me. "Edwin, play something."

Play what? Mother nudged, and the Professor waved me over. I was so nervous as I sat on the stool and played a beginner's piece. The other students and their parents surprised me when they applauded. Mother beamed.

In the weeks and months ahead, Mother pointed me to the upright piano in our parlor to learn the pieces assigned by Professor Kerns. I'm sure I only spent minutes practicing, but it often felt like hours were going by. Practicing at the time was more like a chore, a have-to kind of thing, monitored by my Mother.

Professor Kerns and Mother assured me, "You're making progress." As the months passed by, I began to feel at home on the keyboard. Grandpa's musical legacy had been passed on to another generation.

At about the same time I entered the first grade in grammar school. My teacher was Miss Sally Cook. She was an older, single woman, who had devoted her life to educating and inspiring children. I loved her; we all loved her. "She's so nice."

Besides gently guiding our hands in the writing of alphabet letters on lined paper, Miss Sally instructed us in ways to be safe. "Always, before you cross the street: stop, look and listen." Those four words in large print stood in the chalk tray of her blackboard. Miss Sally also promoted cleanliness. She gave each of us a bar of Lifebuoy soap to take home. "Remember every day to wash your hands, especially if you've been playing outside."

Playmates were hard to come by in the hotel, since I was the only youngster living there. Occasionally cousins stopped by. Most of the time I went next door to our neighbor's house to see Shirley with her bright red hair and freckled face that she could twist in so many funny ways.

Some days I got there before Shirley and her sister Ruth were awake. I just stood there looking at Ruth sprawled in one bed and Shirley in another. Homemade quilts covered both of them. Pants and skirts and blouses were hanging on their bed boards.

On one of those days, Shirley jerked back when she awoke with me staring at her. "Oh, it's you," she said when she realized it was her neighbor, who was around seven at the time. Shirley was closer to ten.

"Come on, get up. Let's play!" I pleaded.

"I had no breakfast. You gotta wait!"

She pulled on some pants and a shirt, and we headed for the kitchen. Galia, her mom, had already fried some bacon, and she'd left a pot of grits on the backside of the wood stove. The stove was warming the room and most of the Kovsky's small, wood-frame house.

While Shirley was eating and her mom was hanging out the wash in the yard, I was messing about the kitchen and touched something red-hot. I started screaming. Galia rushed in and saw me holding up two fingers.

"Let me see here." Galia took my hand and smeared butter on the burnt fingers. "This'll take out the hurt." She cradled me in her arms until I calmed down, and the tears dried.

Shirley prodded me, "Come on, git up! I wanna show you somethin'."

I followed her across the street to look inside a car, a wagon?, that had been sitting there for weeks. It was rusting away beside the creek. We peaked through the windows. We could see the front seats, and in the back...

"What's that...rails?" I asked.

"Them's for slidin' in the coffins."

"Coffins?"

"Don't you know what this *is*?"

No, I shook my head.

"This here's for cartin' dead folks."

I started to run.

"Come on back! No dead bodies here!"

Shirley opened the car on the driver's side and slid into the seat. "Come on, scaredy-cat, open the door!"

I slowly opened the passenger door and looked inside.

"Sit! There ain't no ghosts in here."

I stepped inside, sat down slowly and looked over my shoulder, just in case.

"Oh, no!" Shirley said with alarm.

"Whaaaat?"

"Somethin' moved back there..."

I was ready to jump out when Shirley said, "I'm foolin' you. Nothin's back there."

I stared at her as mean as I could.

We played in the hearse many times. Some days Shirley sat in the driver's seat, other days I did. One day, she imagined, "I'll be?... I'll be a princess, a **dyin'** princess and you?... You'll be my prince, yes! And...you're rushin' me to a hospital... to save my life." I grabbed the steering wheel and off we went.

And another day, "Let's see. Let's... **hurry** to the graveyard, before the **Devil**...can?...dooo... **what**?!" Shirley wondered.

"Before he can **grab** the body back there!" I replied while pointing behind us.

Shirley slammed down hard on the pedal.

Even after the hearse was hauled away, our imaginations never rested.

There came a day, a painful day, when a rift split Shirley and me. Mother had given me a beautiful bird of many colors tied to a stick. I rushed next door to show it to my playmate.

"Look, Shirley!" I twirled the bird round and round. I just knew she would like it as much as I did.

As I held out the stick so she could spin the bird, she cut the string, and I watched the bird fall to the ground. I couldn't believe it! I ran bawling back to the hotel with the bird and stick in my hands.

Mother tried to console me; she said, "Shirley has so few toys." I kept on crying.

A few weeks later the wound did heal, and Shirley and I were pals again.

The hotel was framed originally in wood with a clapboard skin painted a cream color; in the 1940s, red-brick siding covered the building. Sash windows opened into all the guest rooms and public spaces. Daylight passed through the window panes somewhat dimmed by a rusty glaze. The sulfurous fumes from the copper smelters left that glaze on the glass. I often wondered, *Why am I washing these windows? They look the same after!*

I grew up in a 'desert' that spread over 50 square miles. Our public-school teachers told us the miners, starting as early as the 1840s, fired open-pit smelters with trees to remove copper from the raw ore. The smelters' fumes killed more trees. Then came the rains, up to 50 inches a year, that gullied the hills and washed away the top soil and any remaining trees. Back then, no one talked much about protecting the trees or the land.

Barren hills of the Copper Basin, late 1940s

To restore the landscape in the early 1950s when I was a Boy Scout, the common wisdom was to plant kudzu vine, a Japanese import that would "reclaim the land no matter the condition of the soil." Over a period of several weeks, our Troop 13 dug holes in the red clay of a hillside and filled them with kudzu seedlings.

"You're saving the hills, one at a time," our Scoutmaster told us.

Locals now rue the day that we and many others planted kudzu in the Basin. The vine can cover trees and smother them into the sweet by and by. And kudzu is extremely difficult, some say impossible, to eradicate. The hillside we Scouts planted is still swathed in kudzu.

Despite the negative impact of the mining industry, the people of the Copper Basin worked and played, raised families and planned for the future. As for me, I had so much fun sliding down those barren red hills, much to the dismay of my mother.

"I jus' washed your knickers. Stop rollin' aroun' in the dirt!"

We were reminded daily of the smelting operation. Come late afternoon, a huge cauldron, glowing orange-red, moved on railroad tracks across a cliff of decades-old mining waste. From the porch of the Colonial, we watched the container tip and the hot slag from the smelter stream down the black hillside, bathing it in light.

When the smelters' fumes blew our way, the flower garden in front of the hotel often browned out. "Grandma, come look! All the zinnias and marigolds we planted…Look at 'em. They're dyin'. We'll have to start all over again!"

More seriously, lung disease shortened the lives of some of the miners.

It was miners and other company employees who rented rooms in our hotel. And it was the Tennessee Copper Company that paid the wages of over two thousand people in the region known as the Copper Basin. TCC brought prosperous times to our region. You could sense the positive energy in Copperhill when Louis Maloof heartily greeted customers in his clothing store or when "Doc" Tallent swung open his drugstore's door. And you could see it in the shoppers' sprightly gait when they walked down the main street named Ocoee, after the river running through town. Copperhill, less than a square mile in size, also boasted gas stations, food markets, banks and restaurants.

Copperhill abuts the Tennessee-Georgia state line. Copperhill's main street crosses over that line into McCaysville, Georgia, passing by the supermarket, the Masonic Lodge and First Baptist. There's no real separation of the two towns; they are parts of one community.

The moral code in large part was defined and maintained by First Methodist and First Baptist, the largest congregations in the town, with influence throughout the Basin. Some members' peccadilloes occasionally embarrassed the churches, but it became apparent that the rules could be relaxed from time to time without God's intervention.

In my early teens, I was pedaling fast towards First National doing a 90-degree turn on a yellow light. In hindsight I should have slowed down or stopped; instead, my bike and I skidded onto Ocoee Street, hit the curb and both the bike and I tumbled onto our sides. Many cars and trucks were moving down Ocoee - it was a shift-change at the Company - but they all came to a halt.

A policeman helped me up. "Are you all right?"

"I'm okay." I was bruised and scraped, but no broken bones. Mostly I was embarrassed. *So many people are watching!* When I looked more closely, I realized they were genuinely concerned about me. Officer Williams brushed me off and put me back on my bike.

People helping people. That's what I remember about my hometown. In the 1950s, if someone had a problem, usually another someone stepped up with a remedy. Optimism prevailed. We felt good about tomorrow.

In the early 20th century, a new mining technology converted the toxic sulfur dioxide gas into sulfuric acid, a product much in demand by the fertilizer industry. This technique considerably reduced the amount of sulfurous smoke released and made it possible to begin the reclamation of the Basin. In the 1930s, the Civilian Conservation Corps, one of the Roosevelt administration's depression-recovery programs, began to plant trees. Many individuals and organizations have carried on this work. To date more than 16 million trees have been planted, substantially reducing soil loss. The Copper Basin is steadily returning to the green landscape of long ago.

My brother Byron - my half-brother really, we had the same mother, different fathers - he looked like his dad, who was short and red-headed, I looked like mine, tall with dark brown hair. Byron grew up in the hotel, just like me, but nine years earlier. In the recent past he shared with me several of his favorite memories.

"One of the boarders, E. P. Eure, he worked for TVA (Tennessee Valley Authority), he was always raggin' me when I waited on him at mealtimes. He'd fuss about this, about that, like the coffee's not hot enough, the fork's got a smudge on it, the chair doesn't sit right. I'd had it with him! Always complainin'. So, I did it! I marched right behind him… and served his hot coffee and lemon meringue pie on top o' **his head**!

"Oh, yeh, I got a lickin'; but I walked away (his head nodding) with such a **sweet** memory."

And,

"In the basement there was a large hole that opened into the culvert that ran under the hotel. You remember?" I nodded. "Well, sometimes rats crawled into the basement through that hole. Creepy (Byron's pet cat) brought up from the basement a live sewer rat into the kitchen, where Mother was filling up salt shakers. Mother didn't notice the rat until I pointed it out. She jumped **flat-footed** on to the table, a good three feet off the floor! I couldn't do it and I was in good shape!"

When I came along, Byron made it his mission to torment me each and every day. He often pinned me down and told me to "Say 'uncle'." I said 'uncle' so many times. I was defenseless, because he was so much bigger. That was true until I happened on to a solution to end his harassment. Whenever he had pressed me beyond my endurance, his ultimate goal, I would scream. As soon as Mother entered the room I pointed at Byron, who was soundly spanked, no questions asked.

Mother parted with Byron's dad, Walter Davis, soon after Byron was born in December 1930. The marriage that began in 1926 had had several challenges, including two miscarriages. On December 1, Byron was born with a swollen head and a high fever, but he recovered fully. At the time of his birth there was talk of some disease. When Mother's doctor revealed the true nature of the disease, Mother booted the doctor and her husband out of her life.

Not long ago Byron shared with me several framed photographs of his father and grandfather. He paused with the photograph of his dad, and said almost inaudibly:

"When Dad remarried and had children, he told me, 'I have no time for you.'"

I could see the pain in Byron's face and hear the constriction in his throat 70 years after his father slammed the door. In silence, he put the photos back on the shelf of the bookcase and slumped back in his recliner. That was one of the few times he'd ever shared with me his innermost feelings.

Byron knew my dad, and he knew I had tried to bond with him without any success. Byron and I were both fatherless.

Byron and me in front of the hotel with its new porch, 1948

In 1948, Byron finished high school and enlisted in the Air Force. He visited us a couple of times each year. On one of those visits, Byron started destroying his model airplanes. "Why?" I asked. I'd watched him spend so many hours assembling and gluing all the balsa-wood pieces and tissue sheets for each of his dozen models, or was it 15? All of them he'd proudly displayed on the back wall of the hotel's office. "How can you...?"

He ignored me and continued shooting the models with a BB pistol. When the wings were in tatters and the propellers splintered, he looked content. I'm reminded now of a line from the Bible, "Put away childish things." Maybe Byron needed to do it, so he could move on.

Even with all the activity in the hotel, the comings and goings of guests and family, I often felt alone. Mother and Grandma were close by, but the business occupied them full-time; and we all had to keep smiling no matter what, because we were with our guests every day, almost every hour.

Some guests just passed through, staying for a night or two. My uncles, aunts and cousins popped in for lunch, then sped on their way. My dad, a traveling salesman for Olan Mills Studios, also stayed one or two nights, before hitting the road again.

I recall one of his 'visits' with Mother's usual build-up, "Your Daddy's coming!" That time he was eating lunch with several family members when I walked in. He glanced up and said three words, "You're taller." Then back he went to chomping on a fried chicken leg.

Sometimes Mother and I visited my father wherever he happened to be working. One time he invited us to meet him at a hotel in downtown Chattanooga.

We knocked on his door and found him drunk in his undershorts, vomit dribbling down his chest.

"Daddy!?" I looked up at Mother who was holding my hand.

Daddy kept saying to Mother, "Please, help me." And, "I'm sorry."

Mother washed him and pulled out some clean clothes from his suitcase. "I love him," she told me later. "Your dad, he's broken, but he has a good heart."

The three of us left the hotel and walked a while. Similar scenes followed.

No one in my family talked about emotional pain. I don't recall any of my classmates sharing their sufferings, the ones deep down inside. I never told my Mother or anyone else how much it hurt when my Father ignored me.

At the upright piano in our parlor, I spent some private time almost every day. It was there with the hall door closed that the piano and I formed a bond. We became buddies, we became friends. Gradually I began to express myself through the big black box full of hammers and strings.

And I made a startling discovery one night, when I visited the Howell home for supper. Leon Howell co-owned the Ford dealership in town. With awe I looked around the table at the parents, two sons and a daughter, who is still one of my closest hometown friends, happily sharing the meal. The conversation flowed; everyone spoke and no one was in a rush. *This is what a family can be.*

As a kid I begged Daisy to rub my back. Almost every afternoon, when Daisy was taking a break from cooking and cleaning the kitchen, I clambered onto her bed for a back rub.

I was back on the same bed where my Mother birthed me. My Father walked that night to the lobby and signed the ledger with the new arrival: "February 17, 1940, Edwin Hamilton Light Jr."

Daisy's hand felt <u>so</u> good! And she never said 'no,' even though she must have been tired. Mother had no time for it; she was always busy.

"Hey, I've rubbed your back raw," Daisy would often say.

"No, don't stop, not now! Pleeeese keep goin'."

She always obliged. Why, I don't know, since I often teased and taunted her.

One night I waited for Daisy to pass by my doorway. I clicked on a flashlight and pointed it directly into her eyes. She didn't even scream. But much to my surprise, and disappointment, she walked toward me with her hand reaching out to the light!

"Daisy! Why didn't you **scream?**"

But then, she did scream and ran down the dark hallway to her room. The next morning she explained, "I heard when I was young, if you see a light at night, all you have to do is reach out and touch it, and it'll go away." I pondered that for a while, but it didn't quite fit in with what I was learning in public school.

Though short on guile, Daisy had her revenge a few weeks later. Again, it was late at night and pitch black in the bathroom where I was reaching up for the pull-cord. *Where is it??* While I was swatting the air, a voice beside me sighed, "I can't find it either."

I screamed and ran down the hall.

Grandma, Mother and I worked daily to maintain the hotel and its services, along with the toothless Mrs. Ray, who cleaned the guest rooms, and the plumpish Daisy, who busied herself most of the day in the kitchen.

Grandma also spent her days in the kitchen, where she fired up the wood stove at five a.m. She and Daisy prepared three meals a day for guests and family. Grandma's time-out came in the afternoon when she watched soap operas in the early 1950s on our first television set. Grandma believed and breathed every character on the soaps, especially "As the World Turns." That's where she became acquainted with Sally.

After an hour or so of TV, Grandma, usually wrapped in an apron, returned to the kitchen and prepared supper, and then she sat down with us at the kitchen table. "Sally lost her husband today…to cancer," she told us while she dipped cornbread in a saucer filled with buttermilk, her favorite snack. Shaking her head, she asked, "What's Sally gonna do?"

"Sally who?" The rest of us mouthed to each other. Everyone shrugged.

Mother figured it out. "TV."

Mother managed the hotel; she checked in the guests any time of day or night and she kept the books. She also ran the Western Union office. Mother sometimes took a break from her duties on Sunday mornings, when she would attend the Adult Sunday School Class at First Baptist, and time permitting, she also attended the eleven o'clock service. I would also be at that service. Mother insisted.

First Baptist let in the light through tall rectangular windows filled with a milky, brown- and gold-streaked glass. The glass color was copied in the long cylindrical lamps hanging from the ceiling. Red carpet ran down the aisles leading to the altar where sinners confessed and to the preacher's podium. The electronic organ console was on the left side of the chancel, where the choir pews stretched from left to right. Behind the choir, you could see the baptismal pool through an opening in the wall. A glass panel allowed the congregation to watch, while the preacher dipped the repentant.

Our Sunday mornings were filled with prayers, Bible readings, hymn singing and fiery sermons. During the week, I often saw my mother reading her Bible. "Reading it calms me, especially the Psalms," she told me.

My only release from chores came at school. In elementary school, "Sweetie" was my nickname; it was spoken with fondness, so I rather liked it. "Be nice" was another directive from Mother, but I also *wanted* to be nice. Being nice, being "Sweetie," I went a step further and burnished the apple on the teacher's desk. My classmates with surly lips called me "Teacher's Pet." I didn't mind. The teacher liked me.

In my third-grade class we performed a minstrel show on the auditorium stage for all the grades to see. We wore long johns dyed black, and black shoe polish covered our faces and hands. Several of us were wearing short, brightly colored skirts. In a dance routine we 'girls' turned our behinds to the audience and shimmied.

The audience whistled and catcalled, surprising all of us on stage. I noticed our music teacher in the wings, doubled over in laughter. She turned her head and whispered to me, "Look… back." I looked round at my backside where the flap of my black long-johns was hanging open, exposing my white cheeks to the cheering crowd.

I don't remember the year when I started waiting tables in the hotel's dining room. I do remember lifting the brass bell and shaking it with all my might to alert our guests to 'come on down.' As soon as the guests were seated, I collected drink orders, "What would you like, sweet tea, coffee, sweet milk?" Then I began carrying in platters of fried chicken, mashed potatoes and cream gravy, pickled green beans, sliced tomatoes and cornbread. Everything was made from scratch by Grandma and Daisy. When the guests had emptied the platters, I rushed back to the kitchen: "More of everything, more sweet tea and corn relish." The meal cost less than a dollar.

One particular guest, the Singer Sewing Machine drummer, comes to mind. His hugeness spilled over the sides of the chair and pressed against the dining table. That day I'd just slopped the hogs in their pen out back. No matter how much I dumped in their trough, it was never enough. This guest was never content with one plateful; he always asked for more. *Hmm, I should take him to the trough.* I was really annoyed, and I didn't want to indulge Mr. Blob's excess. He noticed my irritation and demanded, "More!" Grandma obliged, while I fumed.

To finish off dinner, I brought in everyone's favorite, lemon pie heaped with meringue. When the dining room emptied, I cleared the tables and sat down in the kitchen for my own meal.

I liked serving meals to our guests because I could listen to their conversations. They came from many different cities, like Atlanta and Knoxville and beyond. I had only traveled a little, so whenever I heard the train's steam whistle, I dreamt about riding to wonderful places.

The Louisville & Nashville train station, a few yards from the Colonial, was busy most of the time with four or more trains passing through daily. Many townspeople dropped by just to watch the passengers come and go. As a boy I watched too, captivated by all the activity: a uniformed man pulling baggage and freight on a large wagon, the hissing of the engine that caused me to jump aside knowing that steam clouds would soon billow, plus all the new faces that spilled onto the platform.

Before my time, the train conductors would signal ahead how many passengers wanted to dine in our hotel. For those who had tight schedules, my family or hired help would walk the aisles selling bag lunches. Mother wrote in the local paper, "Papa hired three colored workers from the Southern Employment Agency in Atlanta: a cook, a maid and a waiter. The waiter doubled as a bellhop, greeting all trains with a bell, shouting 'Colonial Hotel, right across the street,' as the passengers alighted."

The Colonial Hotel and L&N Railroad Station, 1921

In the 1950s, one of us in the family rang the brass bell at noontime for dinner and at 6 p.m. for supper, as well as at 6 a.m. for breakfast.

One morning...

Early on a Sunday morning when I was 9 years old, an explosion rocked the hotel, shattering all the windowpanes. *What's going on?* The first thing I noticed was the window shade bulging over my head. I saw rips in the shade. *It's holding back the glass!* I tapped the floor with my toes. *It feels solid.* Even though I was trembling, I was able to slide out of bed without jostling the shade.

Mother told me later she'd stepped onto the front porch through one of the broken storefront windows. "I couldn't believe I was walking out that window… then… I walked out to the sidewalk, looked round… and saw our rental house had… fallen apart!" That's where Louis Wright, the chief deputy sheriff of Polk County, lived with his wife and two daughters. "The Wrights were pushin' through ceilin' planks… hangin' down on the porch…tryin' to get away from the house."

Beatrice, one of the Wright daughters, had some ceiling plaster in her mouth that a dentist had to remove. The other daughter, JoAnn, a classmate of mine, had spent that night at a friend's house.

Stunned, most of the guests emptied out of the hotel. I ventured outside too, and saw broken glass everywhere. Soon we learned that the windows were also broken on the other side of the Ocoee River, more than a quarter-mile away. *Unbelievable!* And the rental house… beyond repair.

"What was it? What caused the explosion?" Those were the questions on everyone's minds. Hours went by. We swept away the debris inside and outside the Colonial. Fortunately, none of the guests was harmed.

After a day or so, we learned that our renter, the chief deputy sheriff, was the intended target of the explosion. But why? Several explanations exist, one being, the deputy's duties included destroying all the moonshine operations in the county, alienating the bootleggers. Another story: the deputy had offended other people in the community who also resented his conduct. No one really knows the motivation.

Beatrice Wright went on to explain that the perpetrators, "used large fruit cans filled with sticks of dynamite and placed them around the house. Not all of it exploded. One can outside my parents' bedroom did not go off. **Thank** God!"

Another can apparently rolled towards the hotel. It too did not explode, saving others from harm, including my mother who stood by the can unaware of her potential danger, while looking at the remains of the rental house.

In a few months, the Deputy's home was torn down and hauled away. I remember standing on one of the house's support columns, thinking… *There used to be a home here.*

Me on a column, 1949

The Wrights checked into the New York Hotel for a month and then began the search for a new home and new furniture, because the blast had destroyed almost everything they owned. Property owners around town refused to rent to them, because they were afraid their houses would be destroyed. Finally, the Jabaley family offered a place to live, where the Wrights stayed for several years.

Presumably, the perpetrators of the explosion rallied and tried again. They knew the deputy routinely checked the beer joints at night for orderliness. With shotguns in hand, they waited outside the Turtletown Tavern. When the deputy and his friend Bob Rogers, the copper company's security chief, stepped out of the car, shotguns blasted point blank, killing both of them.

Our local newspaper reported the deaths. Three men were arrested… Still, to this day, no one knows definitively the answers to who did it? or why?

The son of one of the men, who may have bombed the deputy's house, was a classmate of mine. Because a new school building was being constructed, we attended classes in the old auditorium that had been divided with eight-foot walls into grade levels. The classrooms had no ceilings. Noise disrupted instruction every day. When the teacher had to leave the room, a student would be responsible for writing on the blackboard the name of any student creating a disturbance.

One day it was my turn to be the tattler. This boy dared me to pen his name on the board while he was bad-mouthing other boys in the room. When I wrote his name, he recoiled: "You shit, you're gonna get it!" I started to shake. "Wait'll I get you outside!"

What have I done? He looked at me hard, but I knew nothing would happen in the classroom. *What about recess?... What's he going to do to me?* I'd heard him threatening other people. It seemed he wanted to be the meanest, toughest of them all. *Maybe he's not so tough, maybe he's just a big mouth.*

At recess he found me in the temporary outhouse behind the school where I was hiding. He flung open the door and shouted, "Get ready to pay!" I didn't move. He raised his fist, and I cringed. We stood there staring at each other. A long minute went by, and another one...

He turned, said nothing and walked away. *I stared him down!* I was trembling...*but I stood my ground.*

In January every year family, usually Uncle Harry and his sons Freddie and Coonie, shot and slaughtered two hogs penned behind the hotel. The three were rowdy, burly guys who worked as boilermakers at the Copper Company.

The three men trussed the hogs and slit their bellies. Large tubs caught the innards steaming in the winter air, as they slid out and were cut from the carcasses. We wasted nothing. All the body parts found their way into a boiling pot or roasting pan.

Harry's sons, at least 10 years older than I, enjoyed giving me a hard time. They'd kid me, poke me and do their damnedest to rile or embarrass me. That day Freddie looked at me slyly as he cut out a hog's tongue and passed it to Coonie; Coonie turned round fast, "Can you handle this?" and tossed it into my hands. I jumped back holding this slippery, slimy thing, looking as mean as I possibly could at my scheming cousins. *What do I do with this yucky mess?* They grinned with bared, clenched teeth as I rushed round trying to get rid of it. I was looking for… *there's a pot!* I quickly slid the tongue into the pot where it would be boiled and sliced for sandwiches. "So there," I spat at the bullies.

On another day, I was eating dinner in the kitchen when Freddie and Coonie walked in. Grandma had just noticed the sprouting of hair on my legs. She embarrassed me when she announced, "You got hairy legs." I was 12, maybe 13.

Soon the bully chant began: "Eddie's got hairy le-egs, Eddie's got hairy le-egs…" I slammed my plate hard with a knife, breaking it in half. "We got 'im again," chortled my tormentors. *Dammit!*

The hotel kitchen was not only where the family gathered daily to eat Grandma's delicious meals; it was also where we huddled to catch up on the latest news.

When you entered the kitchen, you saw two stoves, the electric on your left, and Grandma's favorite, the wood and coal, on your right. Into that stove every morning Grandma slid pans filled with baking-powder biscuits. An irresistible smell… "Pass the butter!"

Behind that stove was a pile of wood leaned against the brick chimney. Occasionally a rat wandered in from the cellar and hid in the wood pile, no doubt drawn there by the bacon bubbling in the black iron skillet. "Where's Creepy?" Fortunately, the cat Creepy kept rodent intruders in check. That cat amazed us all the time; she could creep to the end of a tree branch and catch a bird. No lie.

Beyond the stoves on the left was the entrance to the dining room with its swinging door. After that came the shelves holding all the dining room dishes. That's where I dried dishes from a pan on top of a barrel.

Next you could see the large double-door refrigerator and a storage cabinet. Grandma sometimes kept a six-pack of Coca-Cola in the fridge. I coveted those bottles with the sweet, fizzy stuff inside. When I thought no one was around, I swiped a bottle. Grandma, though, was watching and she refilled the remaining Coke bottles with coffee water and grounds. I'll give her credit: it was a good color match. I snatched another bottle, opened it and immediately spat out the awful-tasting Coke?! No more snitching.

Across from the fridge stood a long table covered with a tough, fabricated wood. We used it for family meals and for prepping platters bound for the dining room. One day, three of the regulars gathered in the kitchen. Uncle Howard shuffled in wearing his oil-stained coveralls with an ESSO patch above the chest pocket; he was sporting his usual mischievous grin. His sister, my Aunt Shine, arrived that day in her new, red Buick convertible, stylishly dressed with a face as pretty as any on *Photoplay's* covers. And good-hearted cousin Raymond walked in dressed in his paint-splattered bib overalls; he worked for the TCC paint crew and had been painting a company house on Cemetery Hill. The three were chatting and munching on ham and collard greens, when the latest gossip turned to…

"The Baptist preacher and his family are up and leavin' town!" Uncle Howard couldn't wait to share.

"They've only been here a year. Why are they leaving?" Aunt Shine asked, disbelief scratched in her brow.

"Their son and daughter…too much sleepin' around!" Howard was salivating.

"Are you kiddin'?. the **preacher's** family?" Raymond asked. With a wave of his hand, "That can't be true."

I jumped in, "I was in church when the preacher told us. I saw the Mrs. wiping away her tears, and... I saw their two red-faced kids."

One day, after everyone had eaten and returned to work, Daisy was washing dishes and I was drying the dishes when in sauntered Mr. Ballew, a gray-haired mechanic at Dickey Chevrolet, in his grease-stained overalls with tobacco juice dripping out of his mouth. Without any introduction, he addressed Daisy, "I need me a wife. My wife died on me, and I need someone to cook and clean." He stood there with a big smile, his head bobbing up and down, expecting a positive response.

Seeing as how Daisy had never laid eyes on him before, she said, "I don't know you! And I ain't interested in **knowin**' you!"

Mr. Ballew fidgeted. He started towards the door then paused, turned round and said, "I'll call again."

Bewildered, Daisy collapsed on a chair.

Daisy had been married and had birthed two children who were now adults working nearby. Divorced and middle-aged, Daisy had a room of her own in the hotel, and her meals, of course. Maybe she had a savings account at First National, but not much else. Daisy had a pretty enough face; her body though, looked to me like a balloon about to explode, and she walked with a limp from a childhood injury. She'd had no suitors at the hotel; in fact, she showed no interest in having a boyfriend or another husband.

Mr. Ballew changed all that. He returned to see Daisy week after week. Finally, she agreed to go for a ride in his Chevy pickup.

After several outings, my Grandma became quite curious - and a bit envious - about Daisy's suitor. "Where do you go in the pickup? What do you **do**?" she asked.

"We drive along on dirt and gravel roads with no place in mind. We go slow. We don't say much. He don't say much ever."

Grandma leaned in, "What **else** do you do?"

"He's teachin' me how to drive, so we take turns drivin'. Then we rest a spell...on the side 'uh the road."

"**And?**" Everyone in the kitchen leaned in.

Puzzled by the family's keen interest, Daisy added, "Well, he cuts my toenails and I cut his."

The hotel was my home school. I learned, I witnessed a lot of stuff, some things maybe too early in life.

On a Sunday afternoon in my brother's room, my Aunt Katie, long troubled by depression took her life. No one heard the shot. After Katie's husband found her, I briefly saw the blood coming out of her neck and the rifle beside her before Mother jerked me out of the room. I was eight years old.

Katie had attempted suicide before. She had thrown herself into the Ocoee River that flowed near the hotel, but a brother had rescued her just in time. After that, she spent several months in a sanatorium.

In our parlor Katie was laid out in a coffin for a whole week, to allow time for family in California to attend the funeral. Every time I walked by the parlor, I shivered. *It's so weird… having a dead person in our living room.* And, everybody was crying, especially Grandma.

I asked Mother, "Why was Aunt Katie so sad?" She looked away and said nothing.

When Katie was a teenage girl, Grandma told her daughter to, "Follow your daddy, but don't let him see you. **I wanna know** if he's with that whore across the river." Grandpa, I've been told, was quite the ladies' man. Katie reported to her mother, "Daddy's with that woman."

Years later my brother said to me, "When Grandpa found out that his daughter Katie had spied on him, he raped her." That revelation tarnished forever my image of a remarkable man.

Two years later I was waiting on tables in our dining room when a boarder, a math teacher at Copperhill High, collapsed on the floor. I had just delivered drink orders when he started twisting and turning; he couldn't breathe. *What's happening to him?* At age ten I didn't know what to do; I turned to the grownups for help. One of the road construction crew lifted the teacher and carried him to his room. Mother explained, "Mr. Johnson was in the Second World War; you know, just a few years back. Johnson has shrapnel in his head; that's bits of metal from a bomb. He could fall down anywhere, anytime. He's resting now. He'll be alright later today." *War...?* I wondered. *Who wants that?*

Another aunt, my Grandma's sister Missouri, visited us several times when I was a kid. I thought Missouri looked really weird. Grandma told me, "When she was born, her skull wasn't closed up, so the doctor put a tight cap on her, and that pulled up the left side of her face." Her left eye never closed. Never.

Most people who met Aunt Missouri shunned her, saying things like, "She looks horrible." And I agreed. I couldn't get past my juvenile judgements. Had anyone taken the time, he would have discovered Missouri to be a kind-hearted and loving person.

And Aunt Missouri couldn't hear well. That skull cap again. When Grandma, Mother and I watched *The Jack Benny Show* on TV, Missouri sat with her ear against the speaker facing us.

Mother was laughing when she said, "Benny's such a clown on that fiddle!"

Missouri was laughing too, but not when we were. *Does she hear what we hear?*

Grandma chuckled when she said, "Look at Benny's dead-pan face. That gets me every time!"

I was watching Jack Benny <u>and</u> Aunt Missouri. It was a double feature, all at once!

Missouri usually stayed with us a week or two, then traveled to another sister or brother's house. She had no home of her own. She had some schooling, but she'd never worked.

The next time she visited, she looked older and moved kind of slow.

Mother, Grandma and I were sitting in the kitchen when Missouri walked in talking about singing she'd heard in her room. "Come on!" She waved for us to follow. We walked into her room and heard…nothing. Looking up at the ceiling she said, "It's Roy Rogers. Listen. He's singing to me!" The three of us stared at each other.

Is she already in heaven? I wondered.

Aunt Missouri spent her last years in a nursing home, heedless of faces or places. She'd had a lifetime filled with the unkindness of strangers and kinfolk. As a kid, I was not charitable to my aunt; now my heart breaks for her.

When I was not visiting with family or doing homework for school, I was busy with my duties, like waiting on tables. One night Mother gave me a new task, "The two construction workers in Room 2 are making a lot of noise, go shush them."

Why me? I was only a kid about to lose my soprano voice, and the two men? They were much bigger than me. Timidly I knocked on the door of the "Honeymoon Suite," the only room in the hotel with private bath. I knocked a second time. Again, I was ignored.

One of the men popped the other with what sounded like a belt and asked, "Do you love me?" *What's going on?* The pop and the question repeated. I thought I heard a whimper from the other man. *Are they playing a game?* I knocked a third time and said in my crackling way, "Quiet, please!" The pop, the question came again and again. I walked away in a muddle.

Puberty and me. I was 12 going on 13 and I was fascinated by all things sexual. In my room I discovered stuff left behind by Uncle Oliver, including books that featured comic-strip characters. My favorite was Moon Mullins and his girlfriend doing it. *Wow!* I was bug-eyed.

The next day I went back to look at the 'comic books,' but I couldn't find them. I searched every drawer in the chest. No books. *Who took them?* As I scanned the room, I stopped at the doorway that opened into Grandma's bedroom. *Did she take them? I bet…she watched me through that doorway.* So much for my sex education.

Later on, Grandma and I were looking out the screen door of the parlor at two dogs mating in the side yard; and that wasn't the first time I'd seen dogs doing it.

One summer night weird noises woke me. I looked out my open window and saw a small female mutt on top of a stack of burlap bags filled with cow manure for Grandma's vegetable garden. The bitch's heat and the moist manure scented the night air. Neighborhood dogs were lining up. One male after another mounted her. Four dogs were waiting patiently in line, well, more or less patiently. All this, just outside my window!

Back at that screen door, Grandma stared at the two dogs and asked, "What are they doin'?" I looked up at her wondering, *Are you kidding? You don't know?* She seemed to really want to know. *Maybe she wants to know if I know.*

"Grandma, they're makin' babies!"

When urgent matters needed to be discussed, Mother and I headed for the family bathroom at the end of the first-floor hall. Numerous times in my youth she and I had been in that bathroom, where I'd heard many a threatening directive.

On this occasion, I was probably 13, Mother took me by the arm and pulled me toward the 'conference room.' I dreaded what was coming. Last time we were here she insisted, "You can't disappear when the dining room closes. You gotta clear the tables, take the dirty dishes to Daisy and dry the dishes as soon as she washes 'em. **Every** day!" *If I only had the guts…*

Why the bathroom for disciplinary pronouncements? It wasn't really a private space, because anyone could hear every word spoken, not just outside the door, but down the hall! Yet that's where serious stuff happened.

This time Mother began, "You're gettin' too big for your britches! You can't just walk outta here without lettin' me know. You can't leave your chores undone. You can't…"

I slugged her in the belly. She couldn't breathe. She couldn't speak. Her hand went up defensively.

I stared at my fist. *I can't believe it! I hit Mother with all the strength I could muster.* I'd felt like hitting her before, but never thought I would actually do it. *If only she'd stop hounding me!*

Mother gasped some more and slowly began to breathe normally again. I looked into her face and saw fright and bewilderment for the first time. She unlatched the door and walked away without a word.

Our relationship changed after that. Mother was less demanding, less dictatorial. She was still determined though, to discipline me. Unlike my brother, who was never spared the rod, I was not struck by hand or switch. Instead, Mother depended on words to direct my path, words chosen now with a little more care.

Grandma treated everyone with kindness and respect. She rarely raised her voice, but calmly made her views known to all concerned.

As a teenager I remember raising my voice in anger at my Grandmother, a rare occurrence. I had just rebelled against doing one more chore. As the only male member of the family that lived in the hotel, I was expected to do my share, and then some. Or so it seemed to me.

Grandma sat me down and calmly reviewed the situation. She assured me, with her hand resting gently on my shoulder, "We all share the work here. That's how we keep this place goin'. Rest a while, then take the slop pail over to the hog pen." Even though it was a loathsome task, I did as I was told, because of Grandma's reasonable and kind manner.

In large part I saw the world through the eyes of my mother and my grandmother. I was with them from birth to high-school graduation. There was no grandfather or father around to emulate.

My two moms welcomed everyone to the hotel, rich and poor, brick layer and company official. And they wouldn't tolerate any kind of racial bias, such as slurs aimed at the Lebanese families who lived and owned businesses in town. I remember some of the boys in school bullied one of the Lebanese boys because of his darker skin. They called him, "Chocolate Boy!" That was a slur akin to "nigger" and spoken with the same ugly tone.

"Don't ever call him that," Mother said.

Mother told me about the three colored workers her father had hired from an agency in Atlanta when the hotel first opened. They were treated like family, working side by side with her brothers and sisters. Mother added, "When Papa died in 1922, Mama regretted she had to send the three back to Atlanta because there was no one to protect them."

When I was growing up, colored folks were not allowed to live in my hometown, save one named Ike Humphries, who worked as an orderly at the TCC company hospital. He was much loved by most people who met him. His job included the disposal of body parts after surgeries. I didn't know where he lived, because he kept a low profile. He had to. There was talk of lynchings in my county.

In the early sixties a group of local men stormed the New York Café in downtown Copperhill and rousted a white businessman and his colored chauffeur out of their seats. "You get that nigger out of our town. Now!" The two men rushed out the door while the vigilantes shouted, "We're keeping our town pure! Clean!"

That attitude has all but vanished with the years. But it was a long time coming.

When Prof. Kerns moved away, I began piano lessons with Mr. Runyon. Runyon was more of a disciplinarian than Kerns ever was. Anytime I made a mistake, like playing the wrong key, holding down the keys too long or not long enough, Runyon would strike the guilty hand across the knuckles with a ruler. *That hurt!*

I complained to Mother, yet she did nothing. I guess she thought I was trying to avoid practicing altogether. However, she must have listened in one day, because she said goodbye to Runyon bluntly. What a relief that was, no more Thursday lessons with Ruler-Man!

There were no lessons for a while. Mother began making inquiries and connected with Miss Mitchell, the music teacher at Copperhill High, who became my next instructor. At our first lesson, she put John Thompson's Book One on the music rack, opened in the middle of it and said ever so kindly, "Play this piece for me." I recognized the notes right away and played the piece. "Well done!" she said. *She's sweet. She's okay.* Before I left that day, I did look round the room, and I couldn't see any rulers.

Not all of my classmates were taking piano lessons. Some boys turned up their noses at any boys who played the piano. That's when I heard, "It's a 'sissy' thing to do." I enjoyed my time at the keyboard, yet I began to feel apologetic for what I was doing.

At our upright piano, besides playing Bach and Grieg, I also played pop tunes I'd heard at the movies. With sheet music in front of me, I played and sang along, "Three coins in the fountain…Each heart longing for its home…Which one will the fountain bless?" Romance in Rome! I ached along with the three that tossed the coins. And, I played and sang the lyrics, "Whenever I feel afraid, I whistle a happy tune… The happiness of that tune convinces me that I'm not afraid." That song brightened my spirits as I imagined I was singing along with Deborah Kerr in the film, *The King and I*. And the list goes on. My collection of sheet music was piling up on top of the piano, along with memories of Hollywood's magical worlds.

In our parlor I switched on the turntable and played 78s. "Stone Cold Dead in the Market," I heard many times; I couldn't get enough of the Jamaican beat. Eartha Kitt singing "Let's Do It!" *Oh my, you naughty lady.*

A group of my classmates in the mid-50s caravanned to the Loews Grand Theatre in Atlanta to see Elvis Presley. The first fourteen rows or more in the large theatre were filled with teenage girls screaming nonstop. They were delirious. You could barely hear what was happening on stage. Between screams, we heard bits of *Hound Dog*, *Crying in the Chapel* and *All Shook up*. The more Elvis swung his hips, the more the girls shrieked, and the further they leaned over the orchestra pit trying to touch him. Desperately so. It was a sight beyond belief; I had never seen such craziness. Elvis **ruled**. The King of Rock and Roll.

In a much quieter place, the Kiwanis Club in my hometown, I played a pop tune of the day, "I Believe," which I'd heard Frankie Laine sing on the radio. The lyrics open with "I believe for every drop of rain that falls a flower grows." Later, "I believe that someone in the great somewhere hears every word." The song topped the pop and religious charts. Today I'm a little embarrassed by my request that night. I asked the Kiwanians to bow their heads while I played "I Believe." Why heads bowed? I was under the spell of Frankie Laine and First Baptist.

My brother Byron brought home the complete recording of the opera *Carmen* on 78s. I enjoyed reading the story, but it was the music that grabbed me from day one. I vibrated with every bar of the Habanera and the Seguidilla. The music was, and is, irresistible.

In my sophomore year in Copperhill High, some of my classmates and I were initiated into the Beta Club, a national honors society. We performed several silly and demeaning tasks on the auditorium stage for the amusement of a hundred or more students and faculty.

First, a club member told us to push a peanut shell across the floor with our noses. *How does this relate to academic achievement?* More 'tasks' followed. For the final humiliation the club chose **me**, probably because I was the shy one. Blindfolded, I sat on a chair in the middle of the stage, my collar turned up and saddle oxfords shined.

The audience started making noises when someone crossed the stage and sat on my lap. The boys in the house whistled and cheered. That someone turned out to be the typing teacher, a young, single and attractive woman all the boys yearned to touch.

"How about a big kiss?" The teacher said loudly. I hesitated. I'd never kissed a girl, a woman, and I certainly didn't want to in front of the whole school. "Do it, you dope!" The boys shouted. "Come on, lay it on!"

I grabbed her and made with the lips like Clark Gable. The audience went wild. I was congratulated afterwards by several students, mostly envious boys. Later I glowed when the typing teacher sidled down the hall towards me and said, "That was a great kiss!"

In high school I played my mother's trumpet. She helped me with all the basics: breathing, embouchure and working those valves. For two years I played in the concert and marching bands. Mother was thrilled. I was following her musical path.

In addition to piano lessons with Oina Mitchell, the music director at Copperhill High, I sang in the high-school chorus directed and accompanied by Miss Mitchell. In the chorus room, she also shared with us the biographies of Bach, Beethoven and many other composers; and she played recordings of their music. "Today, let's listen to the first movement of Beethoven's Seventh Symphony." Afterwards, she asked, "What are your thoughts, your feelings?" Several of us put up our hands. At my turn, I said, "The songlike quality kept me listening." That lyrical quality continues to sustain my interest in all music to this day.

Each year Miss Mitchell prepared our chorus to participate in the All-State Chorus that gathered in Nashville. *I can't believe I'm in the middle of hundreds of voices, singing in the Ryman Auditorium!* Oina Mitchell made that happen every year; she was, after my Mother, the second person who inspired me to be a musician.

There was a third: Nell Rose Ware. She taught me to play the organ near the end of my high-school career. On the electronic organ at First Baptist, I had weekly lessons that led to playing hymns at church services; and in my senior year I played the Sunday service at St. Mark's Episcopal. "You have talent, pursue it!" Nell Rose told me.

I was developing a reputation as a musician, but that didn't seem to matter to most folks in my hometown. The majority only cheered athletes. *Maybe I should be on a sports team.*

In my junior year I tried out for the basketball team. My height of 6'3" was an asset; and I discovered I had the reflexes to handle the ball, move quickly and adjust to whatever was happening on the court. The coach looked me over as the weeks went by and placed me on the varsity squad as a forward. More recognition came my way. I was succeeding in music and sports.

In my senior year, on the second day of basketball practice, Coach Swanson yelled, "Two lines shooting and rebounding from opposite sides, same goal."

Jackie Russell tossed me the ball. I shot and ran towards the goal, where there was a tangle of arms and legs.

Just as I leapt off the floor for a rebound, Ken Sisson rushed in from the opposite side of the court, clipped my feet, and in a flash my chin hit the floor.

I don't recall making any sounds. Shock had silenced me.

"Are you alright?" Ken asked when he saw me spitting out some teeth. Just days before, my dentist had told me, "You have a great set!"

"I didn't mean to trip you," Ken said. "Honest."

The coach took me first to my dentist, Bige Boggess, who told him, "This is too serious. I can't do anything for him here. Get him to the hospital."

I waited on a sparkling clean table in our new hospital. Blood was oozing from my mouth into my stomach. *I'm going to throw up.* "I'm so sorry," I said, and soiled the table.

Dr. Hyatt, the chief surgeon, came in, put his hand in my mouth and pulled my jaw in several directions. Hyatt was Dr. Macho, damned sure of himself. "There's no broken jaw here," he said. An x-ray proved otherwise.

Drs. Hyatt and Boggess conferred. "Take him to Lawrence Fox in Chattanooga," they instructed the coach.

On the 70-mile journey alongside the curving Ocoee River, I threw up numerous times. An hour and a half later, I was admitted to Erlanger Hospital where Dr. Fox wired my jaw the following day.

It took several months for the wired jaw to heal. I could only swallow liquids. "How about a chocolate shake?" Aunt Shine asked. "Yes, ice cream!" I replied. I sucked that shake and others she brought through a straw inserted where a tooth used to be. Dr. Boggess replaced the missing teeth with partial dentures in the months that followed.

I played on the basketball team again, but only for two months. I wanted to conquer my fear of playing on the court, and I did.

1957 was a helluva year. Mother divorced my father and married her third husband. I waved goodbye to high school.

When the phone rang in December 1956, Mother was registering some guests. I picked up in Grandma's room saying, "Colonial Hotel." I heard "Hessie" at the other end of the line and recognized the voice of my wandering Father, still married to Mother at that point. He was addressing her with a nickname she disliked.

"This is Edwin," I said, hoping for some recognition.

"Yeah, put Hessie on." Again he ignored me.

"Hold on, I'll get her." Calling down the hall, "Mother, pick up. It's for you." She picked up and I listened.

"I'm coming home (interrupted by a hiccup) for Christmas," Dad said. *He's drunk again.*

I'd heard Dad's slurred speech often in my sixteen years. I had also watched him in his stupor beg for forgiveness from my Mother, who always helped him clean up, sober up. Then, he did it all over again.

I had begged Mother to say no to him, since he had been such a small part of our lives. My Mother had been my provider, my protector, day in, day out. Dad would occasionally pass through, staying for a few days, then move on to the next town, the next hotel, selling photographs for Olan Mills.

Now the moment I had hoped for… Mother said **No** to Dad for the very first time.

"You f---in' bitch, get offa your righteous ass and welcome me home!" His drinking buddies echoed all his words in gales of laughter.

Mother quickly put the receiver back in its cradle. Two months later she filed for divorce.

I recall a photo, from the early years of their marriage, in which Dad looked content holding me in his lap. Over the next fifteen years, the marital relationship became more and more fractured. Dad's absences grew longer, and alcohol continued to rule his life. In our last family portrait, when I was fifteen, Dad looked detached and distracted.

Hoping to salvage the marriage, Mother had joined Dad on the Chattanooga Portrait Studio circuit, working alongside him in sales. Another dead end. Eighteen years had passed for naught.

After the divorce, Mother looked lost for weeks. She realized in time she needed to move on, now free of any conjugal obligation.

For me it was a bittersweet ending. Mother was now independent, while I had this aching need to connect with my father, to feel his arm around my shoulder and to know firsthand his affection for me... if it existed. Despite all that had happened, I wanted to know him and know myself as well.

After the divorce, Mother wasn't alone for long. Sitting at the roll-top desk in the hotel's office, she picked up the receiver of our candlestick phone and waited for the switchboard operator. I was tidying up nearby and heard,

"Number, please."

"Margaret, 246 please."

"That number's busy, Frankie. Try again later."

One more try and Mother was connected to Henrietta, her longtime friend and confidante.

"I've had two proposals of marriage," Mother began. "Edward, one of our boarders, wants me to marry him and move to Alabama, where he'll work for the

Tennessee Valley Authority. He's the really solid sort, always reliable. And he does admire me. Another boarder, named Bernard, though, is so exciting, so much more passionate than Edward."

I could hear Henrietta's response, even though Mother was holding the receiver tight against her ear...

"Passion doesn't pay for the groceries, Frankie."

Having food on the table, however, was no match for Bernard's 'charm.'

Bernard began boarding at the hotel in late 1956. He was the local Louisville and Nashville Railroad agent. Of an evening, he and Mother would sit together in the parlor talking and watching television. Grandma and I were there too, watching them.

With Bernard in the picture, Mother was so cheerful. She moved about with a big smile on her face and more bounce in her step. A girl again at 49.

My Grandma, though, was not happy with Bernard. She thought him 'not quite right' in the head. I echoed her concern.

A few weeks later Mother announced she and Bernard were to be married, and she left the room.

"What?!" My Grandmother and I said in unison. We were completely opposed to the marriage. "He's not a good choice... Something's wrong with him!... He's unstable." And my brother agreed.

One night Grandma and I voiced our objections to Mother, who vigorously defended her choice. Our voices became louder and louder. The shouting match reached a shrillness that drove two of us out of the room and out of the hotel. I walked up Cemetery Hill and perched on a rock, while Grandma sat on the side-porch swing. Mother remained in the dining room where the argument had begun.

I don't know what the other two were feeling, but I was boiling mad. "How can Mother do something so dumb?" I yelled into the night sky.

I had watched Bernard slump about the hotel mumbling words. He looked afraid and lost. His right eye was always out of kilter.

A week before the wedding, my brother and I refused to attend.

"Oh, yes, you will," Mother screamed, and threatened us with a quick trip to Hell. Her bluster, no, mostly her heartache, persuaded us to witness the ceremony that took place in the hotel's parlor.

After a brief honeymoon, the bridal couple returned to the hotel and to Mother's room next to mine with its paper-thin walls. Each night loud talking awakened me…

Bernard chastised Mother for speaking with the men who resided in the hotel. Mother quickly responded, "I'm the manager. I have to speak with the guests every day."

Bernard kept beside their bed a copy of *The Inadequate Male*. I figured he must be searching the book for more cues to be inadequate. Such was my bias.

The next night Bernard demanded, "Stop talking with Edward Eure and the other men!" Bernard demanded.

Mother tried to reason with him, but he would **not** budge.

On the fourth night, I heard Bernard say, "Now you'll do what I want!"

I sat upright. *What's this?*

"A gun? Where did you get a gun?" Mother asked. "Bernard, please. Put it down."

A gun! I panicked; I couldn't move.

"Not till you promise me!" Bernard insisted.

"Bernard!" Mother probably backed out of the room slowly, her eyes fixed on the gun. I heard her door open and close.

She's out of there!

The next day Bernard left the hotel. Days later some of his family arrived, including Bernard's brother, who explained Bernard had threatened violence before and had spent some time in an asylum. The brother had hoped, "The marriage with Frankie would be Bernard's salvation." After consulting with the staff, Bernard's family took him to a sanatorium in Etowah, Tennessee.

The marriage had lasted less than two weeks.

After her third divorce, Mother walked me again into the family bathroom. This time she didn't reprimand me. She fell on her knees and begged for my help with tears streaking her rouged cheeks.

She's so desperate!

"What have I done wrong? What should I do now?" She assumed complete responsibility for the failed marriages.

I'd just turned 17 and I had no answers. I wanted to relieve her of some of the despair. *What can I do? What can I say?* Extending my hand, "Let me help you up."

Her hopeless look frightened me. She had always been so strong, so confident.

"You were right about Bernard," Mother admitted. "I thought the marriage would work out, and you would have free train tickets to college."

"Tickets? No! That's too big a price to pay."

Mother went on to flourish for over twenty years as the admissions clerk in the new Copper Basin Medical Center, garnering statewide recognition for the hospital's newsletter. And she did all that on her own, without a husband.

In a fourth-grade classroom, Mother was invited to talk about her many years in the Basin. As she closed her comments, she lifted up her crippled arm and explained that it had never been a handicap. "It's only a limitation." She encouraged the youngsters to, "Do the best you can, with what you have."

In 1957, our senior year, I appeared with Faye Adams in the yearbook as *The Most Studious*. The photographer posed us, yes, reading books. Faye and I were flipping pages in hefty tomes, while striving to look serious for the camera. That year the high schools of Copperhill and Ducktown merged to form Copper Basin High. In my copy of the annual, *The Cougar*, my classmates wrote:

"If you ever get as good as Beethoven I'll come and hear you play. Ed."

"Maybe someday we'll get our song written. Love forever and ever, Jane."

"I'll listen faithfully to all your radio and TV broadcasts. Britt."

"You are one of the nicest and friendliest boys I've ever known. Louise."

"You are the best brother a girl could ever have. Sis."

On graduation day in May, I delivered the valedictory speech. Years later, when I re-read it, I was not impressed; in fact, I was appalled by the over-blown phrases intended to inspire our senior class to loftier goals. I remind myself now that I was 17 at the time and those were the words that popped out of me.

Britt, our class salutatorian, and I went to the Senior Prom together, but not as a 'couple.' Britt and I had never discussed our queerness; even so, we knew without a word spoken we were 'brothers.' We had certainly not talked about making a statement at the prom. I couldn't; I was straddling, no, clinging to the fence. Conformity prevailed. Britt, however, was more comfortable than I with his sexuality; he smiled broadly when we entered the gym at Copper Basin High.

Even though my classmates welcomed me socially, I still felt like an outsider. *I have this terrible secret.* In the recent past, I've learned some of them assumed my sexuality and accepted me in the 1950s. *I wish I'd known.* I've also learned of late that my longtime friend Peggy Walter Kilpatrick defended me in high school. "Don't call him that! He's as good a person as you are," she'd told several of our classmates.

For my high school graduation, my father mailed me 13 one-dollar bills and a brief note of congratulation. I guessed thirteen dollars was all he could afford, since he usually blew his paycheck on booze and cigarettes. I did appreciate the gesture, especially since he strongly disapproved of my career choice. "Musicians are destitute," he'd told me. "Be a basketball player." Even though I had enjoyed playing basketball, my heart pulled me elsewhere.

All along the way, Mother had been paying for my music lessons. Together she and I played opera transcriptions for trumpet and piano. I remember 'Ach, so fromm' from *Martha* by Flotow. That was the first of several arias that introduced me to the world of opera.

When I was a senior, Mother took me to Chattanooga to hear my first orchestra concert. The featured soloist, Sigurd Rascher, was a saxophonist, the first I'd ever heard. I was enchanted by the whole event. Eyes, ears and jaw wide open.

Mother, Miss Mitchell and Nell Rose encouraged me to pursue music as a career. Of the instruments I had played, two would occupy me for years to come: piano and organ. I chose piano as my primary instrument, since I had bonded with it long before I played the organ.

In my senior year, I went to the Cadek Conservatory in Chattanooga for piano lessons with Donald Comrie, a Juilliard graduate, who prepared me for my college auditions. He was my first professional teacher. I wish I had studied with him earlier, for I discovered I had much to learn about piano technique and repertoire.

I applied to four reputable schools, and all four offered me scholarships. Miss Mitchell, a graduate of the Cincinnati College-Conservatory of Music, told me, "You should go to my alma mater. It's a wonderful school."

In the fall of 1957, excited and anxious, I climbed on board the L&N train for Cincinnati and my freshman year at C-CM.

In 1960 my Grandmother Lillie reconnected in the Colonial with Frank Sigman. The two reminisced about their friendship decades before when Lillie was married to her first husband.

"You and George chose my name Frank for your child... about to be born," Frank reminded her.

The year was 1908. Surprise! A baby girl, my Mother, greeted the world forcing George and Lillie to alter the name, but not the tribute. My Mother came to be known as Frankie.

Forward to 1960: Frank informed my Grandmother he had buried his spouse after a long illness and "I'm searching now for another wife." He arrived at the Colonial with a list of women he'd known and admired over the years.

Despite the somewhat awkward reunion, Frank succeeded in winning Lillie's heart. Grandma was 79 and Frank 76 when Rev. Duncan married them on Christmas Day, 1960, in the hotel's dining room crowded with family and friends. I trained in from the Conservatory for the wedding.

Grandma and Frank exchanging vows

Soon after the ceremony Lillie, full of fear, climbed on board a plane for the first time and flew to Detroit and Frank's home. "Let's do that again!" she said to Frank and the flight crew when the plane landed.

On a snow-swept Christmas Day in 1962, I visited Grandma and her husband Frank in their Detroit home. They were so much in love, so happy. I watched them moving about the house with the lightness of foot of a much younger couple.

Grandma and my new Grandpa were so excited when they told me about their garden, that was filled in summer with flowers and fruits and vegetables. "Last year we canned green beans and cucumbers and apple sauce and rhubarb," Grandma proudly stated. "All grown right here!"

The following September the love birds mailed me a large box filled with home-canned veggies, and some fresh ones…that were crushed by the jars. Their hearts, of course, were in exactly the right place.

The jars they sent reminded me of the pickled beets, the sauerkraut, the peaches, and all the other good things in the Colonial's pantry that Grandma had canned in years gone by. It was a trip home again, in a Mason jar.

All reports had been upbeat. Then, in their seventh year together, Frank's health began to decline. Frank was 83, and the day came when he needed constant care. During that period my Grandma, who was well into her eighties and also in failing health, returned to Copperhill, where my Mother cared for her. There Grandma learned of Frank's death, a passing lightened by the happy memories of their time together.

"Those were the best years of my life," she told us. I imagine she relished that there had been no more lighting of the wood stove in the Colonial's kitchen at five in the morning.

Grandma survived her husband and lived four more years, almost to 90. "Be kind to old folks," she wrote in her will.

I adored my Grandmother. She had always championed me and my endeavors. She had baked for my birthdays my favorite desserts: blackberry cobbler or lemon meringue pie. She had listened to my ramblings without judgment and with apparent interest. In junior high, when I read aloud a passage from the Bible…"You could be a preacher!" she announced. Grandma was imagining my future work, which had yet to be decided. *A preacher?* I hadn't considered that calling. Her enthusiasm, however, was inspiring; she wanted to help me find the path I would take. Her remark did relate to my future as a professor in a university classroom sharing my love of music. *Hmm, that's a kind of ministry, too.*

In her last four years, Grandma lay silent in a hospital bed that overwhelmed my mother's studio apartment. While she was at work, Mother hired someone to sit with Grandma. Reduced to wordless exchanges, mostly moans, Grandma let us know when she was hungry and when she needed a bedpan. On a visit home, I tried to put a bedpan under Grandma. *I mustn't tear her fragile skin.* I didn't quite succeed, and Mother chastised me on her return.

My Mother's devotion to her Mother was exemplary. She cared tirelessly for her mom. Mother's siblings did assist in various ways; Mother, though, shouldered most of the responsibility. "It's my chance to give back," she said.

When I looked at my grandmother in her barely recognizable state, I recalled that when her first husband died in 1922, she became a single parent at 41 with seven children, ages 10 to 22. The oldest ones helped her manage the hotel, as well as look after the younger siblings. Even so, Grandma at the end of the day was responsible for the family and the business. In the 1940s through 1960 I observed an inexhaustible woman feeding the hotel guests and her family without a single complaint.

Grandma, gone. *So dear to my heart.*

After her passing in 1971, dozens of our extended family gathered in Copperhill to pay homage to the matriarch who had brought comfort and joy and stability to our family for several generations. **Hats off to Lillie Gartrell Sigman!**

When Grandma married Frank Sigman and moved to Detroit in December 1960, she sold the Colonial to her daughter Shine and Shine's son Coonie. They renamed the hotel: "Shine's Lodge." At the time my cousin Coonie was working fulltime as a boilermaker at the copper company and Aunt Shine was operating her Sunoga Cafe. I wondered what they thought would be expected of them at the hotel, which I knew to be a full-time commitment. Shine also knew; she'd grown up in the hotel. In 1963 they closed the hotel because they couldn't make a go of it. In all fairness, the Colonial Hotel/Shine's Lodge may have no longer been viable and needed to be shuttered.

Still, it was a sad day for the family, many locals and many guests and boarders. The hotel had been "the home away from home" for hundreds of people, a community gathering place and the Hood family's business for 50 years.

The Colonial stood silent for more than a year. On a trip home from the Conservatory, I saw a lace curtain blowing out a shattered window, the cream-colored paint peeling off windowsills, the lobby door falling away from the jamb. Wherever I looked, the Colonial was coming apart. *I'm homeless.*

One broken window led to another. Thieves in the night had walked away with Grandma's treadle Singer Sewing machine, several bent wood chairs from the dining room and a few of the cane-bottom rockers in the lobby. Mother wrote, "The roof collapsed. The linen closet fell down from the second floor, its glass panels shattered; washstands fell on top of bedsteads, on top of armoires…" That's not the way to end an era.

I begged Mother to speak with her sister or nephew, but she couldn't, despite being heartbroken. "They own it now. I can't interfere."

"Mother, at least ask them to let you claim some of the furniture. What about the piano in the parlor? We both played it!"

"I can't," she said with tears in her eyes. "It's theirs to do with anyway they want."

My cousin Kay didn't hesitate; she went directly to Coonie, who showed her what he'd salvaged. "I'm going to take home this bed with the little flowers on the headboard," she said. "It used to be in the Honeymoon Suite." Coonie nodded his approval.

In the mid-sixties, the Colonial Hotel was cleared away and replaced by a take-out beer store. Family and friends were mighty disheartened when they recalled a beloved institution now stained by "Milwaukee's Finest."

The beer take-out was a plain, fabricated box sitting atop concrete blocks with four bare walls broken only by a door and a covered drive-thru window. This take-out was the first building you saw as you entered town. You couldn't ignore it, what with all the beer brands competing for attention in blazing neon. *That's a lousy welcome to my hometown!*

Today the beer take-out is gone from that corner too, replaced by a busy dentist's office.

Although the hotel's demise was unfortunate, too many happy memories remain of all that happened inside those walls, to leave it with a negative exclamation point. Family and friends smile fondly when we review the Colonial's 50-year history: Sunday noon when townspeople filled the dining room, when my brother delivered telegrams on his bike, holidays when our extended family feasted in the dining room, when Grandma stretched lace curtains on the side porch, when Tennessee Valley Authority crews noisily occupied the rooms, when we draped lights around the lobby windows at Christmastime… **The smiles go on.**

Acknowledgements

Writing this memoir began some years ago in Santa Fe, New Mexico, where I swapped piano lessons for Glynn Anderson's critiques of my first attempts at recapturing the past. Glynn is a former English teacher at Mt. Holyoke College in Massachusetts. Thanks, Glynn. Next, I taped the voices of my brother Byron, now passed on, and my cousin Kay; they reminded me of days gone by with stories I had forgotten and stories I never knew. Thanks Kay and Byron.

Also in Santa Fe, I joined a critique group led by the writer and artist Sara Eyestone. Sharing my stories and receiving constructive comments helped me to better understand the whole process of expressing myself in words. Thanks, Sara. In Albuquerque, I joined the SouthWest Writers group, where I attended a memoir workshop with several speakers, including Lynn Miller. Lynn was the first person to read my complete original manuscript that skittered aimlessly in all directions. Thanks, Lynn, for your patience and inspiring remarks.

Other readers and editors have included Susan Stiger, Robert Spiegel, Sharman Esarey and Harriet Frye, whose knowledge of our hometown past and present proved invaluable. Thank you, one and all, for your insights and recommendations.

Also, I am grateful to Jack, my partner of thirty years, who's frequently helped me solve the mysteries of operating a personal computer. Did I mention I grew up using a manual typewriter? Task after task, whether it's the PC, creating an account with IngramSpark, obtaining photograph permissions, et cetera, Jack has been at my side, easing the way forward in the birthing of my first book. Many thanks, Jack. I'll say it again tomorrow.

Photo Credits

P. 19, John Eberle, late 1940s, courtesy of the Ducktown (Tennessee) Basin Museum.

P. 35, Turner Photo, 1921

Back cover, Jessica Rath, 2009

Lightning Source UK Ltd.
Milton Keynes UK
UKHW012034040522
402496UK00003B/698